Genealogy 101- Edition 6

Contents

Why be interested in genealogy? The two questions most people want to answer are:

- Where do I come from – who did I inherit DNA from?
- Who else do I share DNA history with?

We are all part of an enormous real life jigsaw puzzle with pieces that are unique only to you and your siblings. What I find most interesting is the stories these people left behind.

I wrote this book to help beginners learn the basics of genealogy and how to build a tree right so that seasoned and professional genealogists will respect you for doing quality work. It can also save you a lot of reworking to get your tree right.

Many people get their DNA analyzed and post a tree without knowing that their tree needs to be built right so it will be found by people who can help them expand it. Why not stack the deck in your favor from the start?

For me, I consider working on my family history as more exciting than watching television, playing video games or keeping up with social media. I am exploring who I am and preserving it for other generations while also helping cousins I have never met build their trees.

My journey to writing this book started with answering the same questions repeatedly for people I met online. Overtime I collected many questions and refined my answers for reuse. Everything I tell you in this book should seem like common sense but even many years after I published my first edition, I still get a lot of repeat questions. Eventually I decided I needed to publish my notes. Everything I tell you in this book should seem like common sense but many years after I published my first edition, I still get a lot of repeat questions. So, the answers are included here, and the teaching begins.

Warning: If you are prone to perfectionism, brace yourself. There will be people you cannot find and there will be errors in the records. Also, things like adoptions, nicknames, surname spelling changes, and conflicting event dates are normal challenges. Get over it now.

As you read you might think that this guy makes it sound easy. Well, that is far from the truth. Sure, I have collected a big tree over the years, but it has never been very easy, and I am still stumped on about 1/3 of my relatively near ancestors. Yes, I inherited two big portions but they both focused on only two of my grandparents. The rest has been up to me over the last 40 years. It's a big puzzle and some of the pieces seem to have been lost.

Set your expectations early. How far on your tree do you want to go? For me, my primary goal has been to record all my ancestors (where I came from), pushing my tree back in time as far as I can. My secondary goal has been recording all the descendants of my ancestors (who do I share DNA with). And, I have gone a tiny bit out of my DNA tree and recorded the spouses of descendants and their parents. This helps to sort out which children go with which spouse. It also helps find connections that cross back into my other ancestors where two siblings from one family married two siblings from another family or a spouse dies, and the surviving spouse marries the brother or sister of the deceased spouse.

Since many of my ancestors lived in small communities, there was a lot of "intermarriage", even down to the first cousin level (oops, it the time it has taken to write this book, I now have to say, "down to brother and sister", it must have been a special situation. And it was in the late 1800s!). Intermarriage used to be a common practice for the royals, they wanted to keep wealth and power in the family. However, I think the peasantry also practiced it. In my tree I sometimes joke that it's shaped more like a double helix than an oak tree. Or, that Maine actual means "my ancestors intermarried nearly everyone" (sorry Maine).

My recommendation to newbies is to start with their great-grand parent's generation and get all those closer related people documented. This will give you a feeling of satisfaction as if you just completed a part of a jigsaw puzzle, which you have just done. When you finish with them you can add another generation and get that same great feeling of completion. Keep in mind that each generation adds double the number of ancestors and who knows how many descendants each of them. It gets exponentially harder, and those milestones of accomplishment get farther apart. Think about it, you have 2 parents, 4 grandparents, 8 GG-parents, 16 GGG-parents, 32 GGGG-parents, 64 GGGGG-parents and so on. At the 10th grandparent level, you add another 2048 grand parents giving you 4.088 grandparents across generations 10 generations.

And, as you get into the 1800s and 1700s farming areas you will find that couples could have 10 to 15 children, all born to work on and live off the farm. A few generations at this growth rate can take a month of Sundays to document.

Most recently I have been sorting my DNA matches by how much shared DNA we have in common and trying to add them to my tree in increments. This gives me much smaller chunks of puzzle to work with in a sitting. But even then, I occasionally come across a name with lots of new descendants making it a very long sitting. To get my small increments, I might choose only people where a common ancestor has been identified, they have a linked public tree, and we share X or Y Centimorgans (CMs). With over 5,000 DNA matches, I know I can never record all of them soon. Rome was not built in a day, and my family tree will not be finished soon either.

When searching for DNA matches, most websites let you filter CM values from 6 to 3490. With a little experience you will start to find CM numbers that hit the sweet spots you are trying to study. 3490 to 2000 typically returns your immediate family. Reducing 2000 to 200 gets you some 2nd cousins, 150 adds some 3rd cousins, 70 adds some 4th cousins, and smaller increments adds the rest of your matches. I highly recommend building your closer tree first. In my tree there are about 500 matches with > 30 CMs. These matches are relatively closer and easier to find. However, about ½ of that 500 are currently not of high interest since those people have either not yet built out their trees past their parents or grandparents or not shared their tree at all. Although I do occasionally email one or two of them when I think we might have data to share. When you get out to 5th cousins and beyond you might find you are dealing with 100s or 1,000s of matches. Not that they are not interesting, it is just that adding one family line can take many hours of effort. I tread into that area only when I need to, such as trying to push the top of my tree back a generation. When I do explore those more distant matches, I take them on in batches of about 2 CMs at a time. This divides up the largest number of matches from the 6 CM to 30 CM into 11 manageable buckets.

Another thing to know is not everyone takes a DNA test. Those who do can choose from several companies. This means that the match you are searching for may exist, but not on the website you are using. Also, not everyone builds a tree while some people do build a tree but then set it as private. And I have seen many trees where people don't know who their grandparents were. Grandparents are one of the best places to start researching upwards because data on younger people is suppressed to protect people's privacy.

One last comment before you embark on a lifetime of tracking down your heritage. You will undoubtedly come across happy stories and sad stories. The sad ones can tear your heart out. History is full of tragedies. Stay strong. It is all about real life.

The Puzzle of Life

As I said before, I look at my family tree as a big jigsaw puzzle. Ancestor connections are the straight edge pieces. They build the frame of the puzzle. Relationships tell you how to fit the pieces together. I relate relationships to the shapes of the puzzle pieces.   Parents fit in with their children and children fit in with their parents. And these pieces start fitting together to build your tree upward along your ancestor lines.

The surnames are like puzzle piece colors. You could group them and eventually fit some of them together. Just like you would spread puzzle pieces of the same color out by color shade increment. You know, this sky blue a just a bit darker than that sky blue. In the case of surnames, you can spread them out by birth dates on a timeline.

Knowing the amount of shared DNA two people have is a new clue. Like the puzzle piece image, it reveals clues that allow you to place the puzzle piece in the right orientation and generally in the correct area of your puzzle. Although, due to the complications of intermarriage it feels like you still need to discern the sky pieces from the water pieces that are showing the reflection of the sky.

So, what does the finished puzzle look like? Well only God knows for sure. I liken it to a pear. If you think about you at the base. You have two parents and each of your parents has two parents and so on upward exponentially until you reach the width of something just a scooch larger than Graham's number. After that point you start reducing in width as you approach the top where Adam and Eve conceived the first children. That gives you one vertical micro slice of the pear. Now add slices for all the other living things and you get the girth of the pear. It is all that simple.

While we are thinking existentially, who do you think you will meet in heaven? Your mom, dad, brothers, sisters, cousins, uncles, aunts, grandparents, great-grandparents... your whole family tree, their friends, and do not forget pets. Will you know anything about them? It is the stories that make each person interesting.

How I Got Started

In the late seventies my uncle was rebuilding his camp house on the lake and came across a box of notes his mother had kept. These were letters and diagrams passed down from several generations of grandmothers documenting their family tree going back about 4 generations. My uncle gave them to my aunt, and she started to figure them all out and added new information she could find. Time went on and shortly after my daughter was born my aunt came to me and asked if I liked puzzles. I said yes of course, thinking she had some to give away (my grandfather gave me quite a few of his jigsaw puzzles).

She pulled out the box of notes and started walking me through our family history and showed me spots that she knew needed research, most especially the mystery of how our Scottish family ended up in Ireland for two generations. And then there were quite a few ancestors that moved away and were never heard from again, at least for these notes. Some letters told the story of coming across the Atlantic as a very large family in 1829 and settling in Quebec. Well, that started my new hobby.

It has been 30+ years now and I still don't know exactly where we came from in Scotland, but I do have good clues to place us in the northern highlands. And, I have found many of the missing ancestors.

The Stories

Finding the stories is part of the fun. I have spent part of many vacations visiting the towns where my ancestors lived. Not just to visit the graveyards but to also visit the historical societies and libraries. That is where you find the obituaries and news stories. In some cases, I met descendants of my ancestors still living in the towns. And I sometimes found the homes that my ancestors lived in. To me, standing where they once stood is a powerful feeling. And I like to imagine how they lived in their time.

As I learned more about my family history, I became more interested in visiting so of the more famous places. My tree traces to three ancestors who came to America on the ship Mayflower. Knowing this, I took my 5-year-old to meet some historians who impersonated the Mayflower people in the reenactment at Plimoth Plantation in Plymouth Massachusetts. We walked through a "time portal" from the visitor orientation center and into the 1620 reconstructed village. It was interesting to meet Francis Eaton and Christiana Penn and learn about their lives. We also saw the Mayflower II which somehow fit the 103 passengers, crew, cargo and supplies for their long and stormy voyage. The story of the main beam breaking on the original Mayflower's journey to America was also interesting. You could imagine the thoughts of the passengers as the ship faced doom and who stepped up to help make the repairs, especially since my ancestor Francis Eaton was a carpenter by trade.

Later when my daughter was a teenager, I took her Bermuda. I had been there before but that was without my family history knowledge. This time I had a few things to look up. Stephen Hopkins was on the ship "Sea Venture" heading to Jamestown Virginia in 1609 when it was shipwrecked at Bermuda (called "the devils isle" back then). The passengers and crew spent 10 months living on the island and built a new ship, the "Deliverance", which they sailed to Jamestown. Hopkins later when back later England and then came back to America on the Mayflower.

Some of My Research Stories

Clifton, Maine

As I started my research I decided to go to the town in Maine where my paternal grandmother was born. It is a small town with only a few buildings in the town center. One of the buildings looked like an old store and was now the town's historical society. I stepped in and told the much older lady that I was researching these four surnames. She stared at my list of names and asked which one I was related to. I said all four. She then explained that these four families were some of the town's founders and she had several newly written books for sale that documented their family trees. I looked over them and bought both. They were in fact useful resources for me. The other thing she told me about was that this weekend was their Sesquicentennial celebration, and I should stay for the festivities that evening and meet some of my probable relatives who still live there. That I did and I learned a whole lot more. Also, while there I visited several graveyards and picked up some more recent data. One grave was for a girl named Aroline Davis. Her father was a road surveyor and have mapped out the main road that goes to Canada from there and is known today as the "Airline" road. I can't help wondering if it should be pronounced "Aroline", especially since the road was built before airplanes came around. However, it is a much straighter line than the Maine coastline if a pilot wanted to navigate by it.

Sawyerville, Quebec

On this trip I started by visiting the cemetery where my family notes said my paternal great grandfather Joseph Mackey was buried in Quebec. It was just a short drive over the border from New Hampshire. My first challenge was that many of the town names had changed to French, and it was more than just adding "La" or "Le" in front of it and maybe an "e" on the end. After a few misses I found the cemetery. It was small, about 100 graves and easy to explore. I soon found it was full of family and started taking notes. After about an hour a man from a nearby house came over and asked me "Qu'est-ce que tu fais" (what was I doing?). He seemed to not understand my very limited French and wrote me a question in English: I have not seen you before, how are you related? I pulled out the family tree sketch I had made and showed him where I fit in. He wrote again and gave me the name of a lady to contact in town who could help me. I thanked him and he continued on his way.

After collecting all my cemetery notes I headed to town to find this lady. She lived in a house not far from the town center and I walked up and knocked on the door. This lady was very old and spoke English. I explained what I was doing, and she invited me into her living room to take a seat. She then left without a word for what seemed to be a long time to leave a stranger unattended in your home. When she came back, she had an overstuffed notebook in her hand and opened it to a page where my name and birth date appeared. She said her husband Chester oversaw family records but had died a few years ago. She had his notes that when back 5 generations to Ireland and a letter about how the family had been forced off their land in Scotland and relocated to Ireland and later moved "en masse" to Quebec.

I asked if I could borrow her notebook for an hour to get it copied and she was glad to let me do it. I think she was also glad someone was finding it useful. The local library was happy to help me copy the notes and accept my US dollars at a fair exchange price. She later donated the notes to the local historical society. I also donated a family bible to them that had a good family tree written in its cover. These documents will hopefully remain safe and accessible to others in the future.

A year later I took my mother and my daughter back to meet this lady and to visit the farm that my grandfather grew up on. The current owner turned out to be a relative and happy to show us around. It was maple syrup season, and this farm was one of the largest maple syrup producers in the region. My daughter got to taste maple syrup ribbon candy made by pouring some syrup onto the snow outside the sugar house. She also learned how maple syrup got its brown color.

Baltimore, New Brunswick

It was time to explore my maternal great Grandmother Lucy Steeves' birthplace, so I headed to New Brunswick to explore the cemeteries in and around the small town of Baltimore. As I was exploring a cemetery in nearby Hillsborough there was a sign for the Steeves Family Historical Society with an address that was a block away. I drove there next and found the parking lot full but there was a sign on the door stating it was closed for a private event. Disappointed, I started to walk away when a person came out and asked if I was there for the Steeves family reunion. I said no but that I was related to Steeves and looking to learn more about my family history.

I was invited in for a wonderful potluck lunch and to view a very large mural rolled out with what seemed like several 1000 names on it. The family historian took me to the spot on the mural where Lucy Steeves fit in, and I quickly started taking notes about her ancestors and descendants. I also filled in the tree down to my current family and left my contact information.

On that same trip I visited the county historical society and several other cemeteries to collect a lot more information about my family.

A few years later I heard from them again as they were planning a family reunion to celebrate 150 years since the first Steeves settled in the town. So, I had a year to collect my Steeves brick walls and then attend the reunion. It was a 4-day event with over 6,000 people related by DNA. I had an amazing time, and I resolved many of my questions. I learned that the Steeves had originally come from Germany and settled in Pennsylvania. Ben Franklin came to them one day and asked if they would be interested helping settle the land that was recently acquired from France and now called New Brunswick. They took him up on the offer and sailed on a ship named "Lovely" up into the Bay of Fundy to the town of Hillsborough. There the family resettled and has been ever since.

I not saying your exploration trips will be as fruitful as mine have been, but you never know if you do not try. Just walking around the towns and seeing the homes where my ancestors lived is often enough to make it a great trip.

Finding Your Roots – Public Broadcasting

My wife and I watch the PBS series "Finding Your Roots" often (surprised?) and I occasionally see names and places that might match my own tree. The first was in the episode with Courtney Cox where some simple research determined she was my 9th cousin on my mom's side. More recently I traced Michael Learned, who has not been on the roots show, but we also like to watch old episodes of "The Waltons". She traced to be my 9th cousin on my dad's side.

What Happens When You Die?

If you are going to put so much effort in, you should think about what to do with the data. It is like crocheting a giant quilt, you need to figure out where it will go. For me, I periodically upload my validated data to various websites so it can help others. You might also be thinking about who in your family you will trust to take it over and "finish it" if you die before it has done. ☺

Ok, time for some real training.

Understanding DNA

Every person has DNA that is unique to them. At the moment a male sperm fertilizes an egg in a mother's womb, the male DNA carried in the sperm mixed with the female DNA in the egg to create a complete blueprint of God's new person along with the instructions to construct them. If you were to test that DNA, you would know what sex they will be, the color of their eyes, their heritage, and lots more.

For tracing of ancestors, cousins, and such we are only concerned with a very small segment of the DNA spectrum. If we were trying to tell the difference between two brothers or two sisters, we would include a few more segments but still not many compared to what is there.

Males can trace their Y-dna up their male ancestor line all the way to Adam. Female can trace their Mt-dna up their female ancestor line all the way to Eve. Of course, no one has ever traced their tree back that far but deep studies of DNA suggest it is theoretically possible.

Y-dna and Mt-dna are great for focused tracing up paternal and maternal lines (called direct lines) and they both contain subgroups called "Halpogroups" that can pinpoint the regional area where your ancestors lived many centuries ago. However, for general family tree research, Autosomal DNA is used.

Everyone has Autosomal DNA. It can be used to identify if two people are related to each other. And, with good accuracy it can predict how many generations their up their direct ancestor lines to where they share a common ancestor. DNA has helped genealogists fill in many of the gaps where documentation has been lost or was never created.

Unless you are an identical twin, each person is unique and inherits a slightly different amount of DNA. Because of this you might find a few matches that your siblings cannot find, and vice versa. Collaboration is recommended to sort them out. Also, your parents will have different DNA and a one generation advantage for finding matches.

My mother's DNA links to all her known 1st cousins, but my DNA is missing some of them as 2nd cousins to me. Nearly as I can guess we are different by about 5% and those seem to be mostly in the closer cousin area. I am guessing this is a normal thing since we do not inherit all our parents' DNA. I like to think God was in there weeding out the bad and nurturing the good to build me into better person. Hopefully, the devil is not there helping too.

Having your parents' DNA test results and probably even your grandparents will help find these gaps. However, do not feel all is lost if you do not have other close relatives to collaborate with because it generally only affects a few matches.

In my case I found a lot of dead ends in Virginia back in the colonial days. Then one day while studying my Mom's DNA matches, I found one who had moved from Maine to Virginia and working down from him I connected most of my matches in Virginia.

The Process

Building your family tree is all about finding the information. You should be looking for names, dates, and places of each person. A good way to start by querying your immediate family. Get their full names, places of birth and birth dates. If they have any records of deceased relatives, get those too. Then it is on to research on the web and in libraries, churches, and historical societies.

Search using the clues you have. Keep adding validated tidbits as you go along. Update dates that only display the year to include the day, month, and year.   Refine names from initials to become full names and nicknames. Refine locations to become the town, county, state/province, and country. Add marriage dates and locations. Add Christening dates and locations. And collect stories about their lives. What records did they leave behind? Look for wills, court records, newspaper articles, etc. Tidbits of what was going on in their town could also be interesting.

When searching on-line I find myself toggling between multiple websites. Ancestry.com is my home base, then FamilySearch.org for some records and FindaGrave.com for other records. Why toggle? Well finding someone on FindaGrave.com is difficult if you do not have date of death or burial place information. But it is generally good with stories and relationships that are not recorded elsewhere.

FamilySearch.org is difficult to find people if you do not have enough name and birth date information. But it is generally good with event records and snippets of family trees that are not recorded elsewhere.

The bigger genealogy websites seem to have the larger collections of family trees, great DNA tools and access to correspondence with other people, which you need to solve your tougher problems.

It is also useful to examine a person from various views. Although it is a bit redundant, I will often find new data looking at the same records from different views such as the person themselves, or as their father, their mother, their spouse, and their children. Why? It is something to do with the way records are stored and the fact that misspellings occur so often.

An example would be that while searching for records tied to a person's father there is nothing new. Then searching for records tied to a person's mother turns up that same list and maybe a few new records that just might contain the gold you were looking for.

Also, look at other collections of data. One will sometimes have much more detail than another. You might pick up a middle name in one file and a death date in another. I will sometimes look through as many as 10 trees for the same person just to find a few more pieces of data.

Another thing to watch for is people's middle names. They are often passed down from grandparents, which can be a clue to a relationship. However, having a middle name that matches a grandparent's last name, or a first name that matches a grandparents' first name does not guarantee they are related but, but it certainly helps to build the case.

Probably the most challenging part of the process is finding descendants. For ancestors it is clear and certain that two parents should exist. That is the way God made us. But when you are searching for a person's children there is uncertainty. Did they have children at all? If they had children, how many did they have? There are precedence's to how many children a mother or father might have.

The greatest officially recorded number of children born to one mother is 69. The wife of Feodor Vassilyev (b. 1707–c. 1782), a peasant from Shuya, Russia, in 27 confinements she gave birth to 16 pairs of twins, seven sets of triplets and four sets of quadruplets. For men it gets even harder. Moulay Ismail ibn Sharif (b. 1672– d. 1727), Monarch of Morocco had a harem of 500 women and registered 525 boy births and 342 girls. In total, an observation was made of 1042 children, then eventually after his death it was determined to be a total of 1171.

And, before you check that box that says, "died young and never had children", the youngest parents on record were in China in 1910. He was 9 and she was 8. Also, when the software asks if the person is still living, be certain before you say yes. The oldest person ever was Jeanne Calment or France who lived 122 years and 164 days. When asked her secret to how to live that long, she said, "don't die" and smiled.

So, never say never. For the record, the largest family in my tree so far is 16 children by one wife. The youngest to have children was 13, and that was almost year after their marriage. The youngest marriage was two "kids" that were 11 years old. I had to clean my glasses and re-read the marriage certificate to be sure. My parents would not have let me get married at that age. I was not even allowed to date until I was 16. Finally, my oldest ancestor lived to be 105. I will beat that that for sure if I do not die sooner.

Over time I have been building my tree using two plans of attack. Every few weeks or months I look for new matches and enter what I can do to either link them into my tree or record enough of their tree to possibly link them in at some future date. Since they are DNA matches, they will eventually link to my ancestor tree. About every 6 months to a year, I look at my ancestor tree for the youngest dead end and research it in hopes of resolving it and pushing that part of my back a generation or two.

30 years ago, my goal was 6 generations back in time, now I am shooting for the ancestors born in the 1400s which is 10 generations back and just past the limit that DNA can take me reliably and not so far into the area of uncertainty of relying on other people's research. It can be quite disappointing to record several days' worth of family records and then learn a few years later that you are not really related to any of them. Having a cut-off for your tree also helps make it easier to manage. I sometimes feel my cut-off date is too far back, but I made my bed, and I will lie in it.

Besides, researching every ancestor back that far is a daunting task and I still have many gaps in the 1800s to fill in. But new data is always showing up, and those gaps have been slower resolved. I'm not sure if I will ever get them all. BTW, when I must disconnect a segment of my tree because of a new discovery, I do not delete it from my database. I learned early on that sometimes those same people end up connecting back at a different point in my tree.

Here is how I am building and managing my tree. I did not invent the process, I learned the techniques from a professional at a Roots Tech conference. The process goes like this:

1. My primary focus is on building a tree of my direct ancestors. This is what I publish. I do not publish descendants of my ancestors to save space and to not get questions such as "Can you tell me more about so and so, your 10th cousin, twice removed?". Instead, I get only questions about my ancestors.

2. I tag everyone related to my in any way as either "ancestor", "descendant", or "descendant's spouse". People who are not related to me remain untagged. This way I know whether I am building my tree or wandering off track. It also helps me know when a DNA matches' tree first intersects with mine.

3. I research every new entry upward to determine if they link to me or not. If not, I will leave them in my database in hopes that they will someday link in.

4. If I see that same unlinked person popping up several times in other people's tree, I might add them as speculative hoping they will eventually link it. And if someone has a familiar surname, lived in a familiar town, or were buried in a familiar cemetery, they are also good candidates to add to my database. Each time I subsequently run into one of my speculative entries, I will try to add a generation to them along with the descendant that brought me there so they will grow in the direction of maybe connecting to my tree someday. In most cases these "islands" of unlinked people do eventually connect to my tree.

5. When adding new people, I research them upward to find where they connect to my ancestor tree and then document them downward in a direct line. I do this for my DNA matches and also their spouses.

6. My secondary focus is on validating my tree. I do that by overlaying the trees of my closer DNA matches onto mine. I am only interested in the direct lines from a DNA match to one of my ancestors. In many cases there is more than one common ancestor per DNA match. And bonus of the overlapping the DNA match trees is they occasionally have the answers I have been looking for to resolve my many brick walls. In fact, a lot of the growth in my ancestor tree has come about from the trees of my DNA matches.

Tip: if a person you are tracking a person who was an immigrant, record at least one more generation back into their country of origin. This can help others find them and maybe grow your tree along that line.

When you build downward along descendant lines, a new rule becomes important. Pay attention to marriages so you can trace your DNA inheritance to the correct children. DNA has given a whole new meaning to "blood relatives".

I have found that I do much better research by following a set pattern each time I explore someone's tree. This way if I get interrupted or must set my work aside for a few days, I can get back where I left off faster. My preferred process is to explore upward on the first line to at least 10 generations of when it ends. If I find a match to my tree I will work downward from there and update my tree with their direct line. As I add spouses, I work up their line in the same way as I do with a DNA match and for some reason more often than not I find that they too link into my tree so I them work downward on their tree and update my tree with their direct line back to where I started on my DNA matches tree. It's time consuming but almost always rewarding for improving my tree. Best part is that I occasionally find a DNA matches tree goes higher than mine and I can expand mine upward.

Finding your Biological Parents

If you are adopted, the process of finding your biological parents is almost the same as the process described in the previous section except you don't yet have an ancestor tree. I recommend approaching it this way:

1. Find your closest DNA matches and overlay them in your genealogy database. You only need a few generations and might need to build their trees up to where they are useful.
2. Pay attention to who their common ancestors are.
3. Use these rules to narrow in on your target pair of parents:
    a. A DNA match for brother or sister share your parents (bet you knew that ☺)
    b. DNA 1st cousins share your grandparents (aka 1st grandparents)
    c. DNA 2nd cousins share your great grandparents (aka 2nd grandparents)
    d. DNA 3rd cousins share your 3rd grandparents
    e. And so on up the tree.
4. Once you have identified a probable common ancestor, build their descendants tree downward and your parents should reveal themselves.

Yes, it looks easy but finding data on living people is tough. However, if you can collect enough data to narrow down to a probable target, you can try contacting a few DNA cousins and they might help you fill in the gaps.

Linking in DNA Matches

The challenge with DNA matches is you generally do not know a lot about them, and they might not know a lot about themselves. I often come across a DNA match where the amount of shared DNA we have is <150 cm so they are at least out at the 3rd cousin level. This can get complicated more if the person only knows their parents' names and birth dates.

The way I deal with it is to do research and try to build up their family tree in my database. Not their whole tree, just enough to get back to the late 1800s where on-line records are more plentiful. Usually that is to their grandparents' level. Most often I can then use on-line tools to find those people's records and associated family trees to find the paths to our one or more common ancestors. I then document only those direct descendant paths into my tree.

I will not live long enough to record every descendant path from my tree, especially for those starting back 10 generations or more. It's tens of thousands of records.

However, the more closer DNA match descendant paths you record, the easier it gets to find paths to your more distant DNA matches.

Another thing that can make research easier is to memorize your ancestor names and locations. I like to take out my direct ancestor tree and refresh my memory at least once a year. It's hard to remember them all but it's nice if a name looks familiar when you are researching. Poking into the name a bit deeper will often yield new clues.

Sharing Data

Part of building your family tree often includes sharing your data with others. Sure, there are great on-line resources for records and to view _other_ people's family trees. But are those trees accurate? And records might also be misleading. Discussions with others can often help clear mysteries.

For example, a person working their way up their tree may be stopped at a certain ancestor and just cannot find any information about their parents. Another person might have those parents and not be able to find any children. However, if the two people are DNA related and start to compare notes, the answer might become clear. I have seen many cases where it was as simple as knowing that the spelling of the surname was changed between generations. Each person had a clue but with was not until they compared notes that the answer became clear. One place in my tree, the name Steeves became Stief. I do not think I would have stumbled onto it.

When people communicate with others it often turns out that one person has the answer to another person's mystery. So, even as a confirmed introvert, some email communication with carefully targeted strangers can yield good results. I recommend trying out a message board or two, it is not cheating on solving the puzzle. Think of it as polling the audience for a lifeline.

One of the things I like to do when I think I have data that someone else does not have is to send them a message with a link to the data. I send out a lot of these messages to my DNA matches who have only a few names in their tree or what looks like a dead end for their research. My hope is to help someone else build their tree which might later help me find where the DNA matches I am looking for. Most often I never hear back from them, which I am fine with since I am a stranger to them. But every now and then I will get a heartfelt thank you.

Descendant Trees

My descendant trees tend to be mostly direct lines to my DNA matches. I ignore other siblings but do pay attention to other marriages and their siblings if the DNA trail goes there (I.e. a spouse who inherited my ancestor's DNA remarries and has more children).

The exception is at my great-grandparent's level, for them I have tried to record all their descendants. This data is great for family reunions.

Another case where I will trace all siblings is when I am helping an adopted person figure out where they fit in my tree and possibly identify who their birth parents are.

People Records

People have been recording who is who for many centuries. You might remember that the only reason Joseph and his very pregnant wife Mary were traveling 65 miles for five days over the mountains from Nazareth to Bethlehem was to be counted in the census. Records of who is who help maintain our law and order. Bad guys cannot just switch towns and start their lives over. And they keep track of who paid their taxes and who did not. However, records are hard to preserve. They decay over time, the repositories flood or burn down. Or in wartime the enemies can destroy them. Some records are just never recoverable. Storing duplicates in separate geographical areas can help. Just look at the Dead Sea scrolls.

One of the great things about these old records is that if you are lucky enough to trace a name back to before the 1800's there are ample records online to get you back much farther, if you trust other people's research. I have found that older records have had much more scrutiny and tend to be more accurate. But they do change from time to time are new data is discovered so beware. It is because of this uncertainty that I do not bother to transcribe them into my tree unless there is a compelling reason to do so. I know where to look them up and that is often good enough for anyone born after the 1400's, which is well beyond my circle of DNA matches.

Spelling

The best writers 100 years good were not as good at spelling as most 5th graders are today. Many old records are more phonetically spelled than what our generation has defined as "proper". Keep in mind we have not yet settled on the spelling of words like "canceled" which is also correct as "cancelled". And I got marked down in college for spelling the color "gray" instead of "grey".

It is best to leave the old records exactly as you find them. Translating them can sometime change their meaning. Some words meant different things back then as compared to now. In the bible it talks about the parting of the red sea. But there was no "red" sea back then. There was a sea called the "reed" sea and scholars believe that the name was changes when the bible was transcribed to English from Greek.

If you are compelled to correct old documents while transcribing, try to keep the original intact and put your corrections in <brackets> to record how you are interpreting it.

Leaving names the way they show on a document will also help with searches and linking to others. You might correct the name Smithe to Smith but someone else might be translate to Smyth and you would never connect.

Probably the biggest challenge you will face is lack of written records and records in foreign languages. If you are like me, some of your ancestors came from other countries. Since I am in North America, almost all my ancestors came from someplace else.

Different cultures started documenting people at different times and in different ways. Early writing dates in 6600 BC are with cave drawings and such. In 3500 BC we see forms of messaging chiseled in rock. In 480 BC we see stories being recorded on papyrus scrolls. In the early 1800s there were still a lot of cultures with only oral history. For example, it was in 1825 that the Cherokee Nation adopted Sequoia's written text for their communications. And today we see written records about people being kept in almost every country.

But even with written text there were still cultural differences where not all people were documented. This was mainly based on social status. Early 1800's census records in the USA show native Americans and slaves documented as numbers by classification.

Then there is language. For me, many of my ancestors came from English speaking countries. But not all. And, my wife's ancestors are mostly from Greece and Czechoslovakia, two places where many records were lost to war and natural disasters and not very many have been translated to English.

My dad's ancestors lived several generations in the Eastern District of Quebec where records in English are ample, but the online versions have been slowly changing to replace the English names for places and people into French. I am a big believer in not changing records and I find it frustrating to have historic town and people names being converted to their present-day French names. It is not so bad when the spellings are close in both languages but that is not always the case. However, it is their country, and they can do as they want to please their population. The adage by George Graham West applies: "History is written by the victors". At least they have not chiseled new gravestones. My ancestors stone still says "John" not "Jean" although "Parkhurst Cemetery" is now known as "Cimetière Parkhurst". With a little language experience, I can deal with it. On the good side, if I want to visit these places, I need to know their current day names to find them on a map. And knowing a bit of the language helps greatly in getting to know the people. Then also, knowing the name for the USA in their language also helps too. I remember as a kid staring at the monitor in a train station in Quebec wondering which train was going to the USA. It turned out to be the one that was going to "Etas Unite".

To research in countries of different languages you have a few choices. One is to learn the language so you can work online. In some cases, you might need an alternate keyboard to type in your queries in the proper text. And be aware that some cultures write right to left or top to bottom.

Another option we have already discussed; post your question to a message board or correspond with someone who speaks your language in that country.

My favorite option is to plan a vacation to the country of interest and reserve time to visit the town's historical society and churches. This has worked well for me. Of course, I still had to learn some language skills. And, even in cases where I did not come home with a lot of new records, I did get to walk on the soil, see the sights, and taste the foods. It always seems more special when you know your ancestors once lived there.

I have very fond memories of eating goulash by the fireplace in a pub in Slovenia and chatting with the locals about life there. And my trip to Greece was unforgettable. Who does not like Greek food, sandy beaches, and dancing outdoors?

A translation tip: Point your smart phone at the screen and use a language translation app like "google translate" to reveal what it is saying in English.

Numerology

As you spend more time looking at people's records you will undoubtedly start to notice that people were born, married, or died on the same month and day as you, your spouse, or your children. At first you might think this is an amazing clue from God. And maybe it is since God did build our world. But if you study numerology, you will know it is more likely just coincidence caused by simple probability. There are 365 days in a year and the probability that any two people in a group of 124 people were born on the same month and day is 99.999%. Check it out. It is called the Birthday Paradox.

In that same area of thought there is a theory I was told once that mothers have more boys at times or war and more girls in peacetime. This was Gods' way to bring balance back. I have never seen numbers to prove it, but it is an interesting thought. Statistically we still seem to always come back close to a 50:50 male to female ratio.

And I wonder if how we select a mate is genetically driven. Could our DNA be controlling our pheromones such that we are attracted to or repelled from each other? Maybe some scientist will write a thesis on it. I recommend that they publish it first in the April 1st edition of the Harvard Lampoon just to be on the safe side.

Something that is not numerology is the fact when a husband and wife and sometimes the children all die on the same day. This is usually due to diseases such as smallpox, typhoid, rubella and such that had no cure back in the days.

I had a whole family in my tree die in Lake Champlain. I digging deeper I discovered they were traveling home in winter across a frozen section of the lake when their horse and buggy broke through the ice. Sad story by also got me thinking about how often I have driven seasonal on ice roads.

Recording People

When you are recording people, you need information about them. Ultimately you should know who they are, where they were born, and where they were born. Name, time frame, and locations are all helpful data in genealogy. Sometimes you have very little. For example, you might only know a spouse existed because the person you do know about had children. How do you document them? For me, I let the fact that there are children be my signal that a spouse must exist. I leave it at that and do not create a record for that spouse yet since I do not know who they are. I might find a marriage date, but still no spouse. However, if I know a given or maiden name, or place they came from, I will go ahead and create a record for them and guess at their birth date. It all comes down to having enough data to justify creating a new record.

For me, if I have a first or last name and at least an approximate birth date, I feel comfortable creating a record for a person. Think about it, if you have two siblings and no idea who the parents are, you can create a father using their last name and estimate the father's birth date by subtracting 20 years off the oldest child. There is not enough information to create a record for the mother, although you do know she must have existed. Just as you know you have ancestors going back many more generations than you have traced so far. Records with the people as "unknown" add no value to the process and waste peoples time since there is nothing to learn when you open the record.

Having a death date makes the case stronger. Having a birthplace, death place, and burial place make it even stronger. Then adding christenings, immigration records, census data, parents, children help tie the bow on assuring this person was real.

And I strive to record all parents as pairs. This has many advantages and strengthens the identity of each. One advantage is it is sometimes easier to find a tree on-line in cases where one spouse comes up "not found" but the other spouse has a tree.

I very often see where people have recorded themselves or their mother by their married name. I get it but in genealogy we prefer to record people by their birth name.

We must also be aware the genealogy is worldwide. It would be helpful if you included the country in the location data for each record.

Surnames (last names)

Throw out any notion that someone 400 years back might spell your surname the same way you do. Spellings change over time as people move to new locations and convert to new languages. Also, many people did not read or write in the old days. You will need to widen your search to try various phonic spellings. And even that might be thwarted by the fact that long ago the surname was not as important in life. Anyone remember John the Baptist's last name? How about Jesus? I used to think his last name was "Of Nazareth". Many people think Jesus's last name was Christ, but that is not true. Christ is the title given to him when he was baptized. It translates to mean "the anointed one".

In England, surnames became common in the 1400s. Nicknames, descriptive names, place names, clan names, and occupation names eventually became surnames. Examples of occupation names are Baker, Smith, Cooper, and my favorite, Brewer. For slaves, many of them took on the names of the family they worked for, making it much harder to trace them back farther by paper. DNA is the better route in that case, but it also gets harder to use after 6 generations back, although the basic area of origins can still be discerned.

So, with the variation in spellings, what name do you use? I like to go with the name on their records or tombstone. And as awkward as it seems, sometimes it is spelled differently between siblings. More often I see it change between birth and death.

If you do not know a surname, please just leave it blank. Refrain from entering "unknown". Also, some people like to capitalize the entire like "SURNAME". I personally prefer capitalizing only the first letter and the letter after an apostrophe name like "O'Surname". And there are those who like to put the surname in brackets like "/Surname/" which causes other people extra steps to copy around or remove them. To each their own, I guess.

Missing Surnames

There are cases where you might not know a person's surname. If it is for a father, in our western culture it is typically the same surname as the child's. And vice versa if it is for a child, it's the same surname as the fathers.

But what if you do not know the father's or the child's surname? Then you might use the surname "unknown". Most software programs will not consider the surname "unknown" when looking for duplicates, which is a good thing since you are likely to have plenty of them.

Another case where you might need the surname "unknown" is for a spouse where all you know is when or where they were born. My preference is to use their married name and add a prefix of "Mrs."

Why do I make such a big deal about this? Please do not use the "unknown" frivolously. If there is no real information being added, just say no and not create the record at all. Empty records add no value to your tree and just get people's hopes up thinking there might be some real information where there is none.

Putting the right data in the right places is important. Avoid putting text into places where dates should go. Also avoid putting in "non-value added" data such as:

- Creating parent or spouse record that has either "unknown" or nothing of value added in it. Having no record is easier to deal with than a useless one.
- Putting "unknown" or "?" where a date, given name or location should be. Leaving a space blank implicitly says unknown and is easier to find.
- Putting a before or after date that references a known date. For example, a baptizing date is known, and birth date is entered as "before baptizing date". Or a death date is known, and a burial date is entered as "after death date". These non-value entries mask the need for needing to add the real dates someday.

Most data for records comes from different sources and are usually created by different people. Birth dates come from doctors, midwives, and parents. Baptism records come from churches. Death records come for coroners. and burial records come from graveyards. All of these are prone to human error. This does not mean someone built a bad tree. They build it using the best information they can get.

When you build your tree, try to build it to at least the great grandparent level. Put in middle names and use birth names for the women. This will make you tree ready for others to help you expand it upward.

Name Prefixes

Some prefixes are simply formality. Example Mr. Mrs. Ms. It is best to leave these out unless there is a special need for them.

However, some prefixes are titles and help to determine a person's role in life and can help narrow down who is who. Examples: Captain, Reverend, Doctor, Deacon, King, Prince, Sir, Count... or, Queen, Princess, Lady, Baroness...

It is also respectful to them; they earned their title, and you should keep it as part of their legacy.

Given names are plagued by four factors. First, in some family's people will go by their middle names instead of the formal first names. And many people will go by nicknames. Many Roberts go by Bob, Johns go by Jack, Charles' go by Chuck, Mary's go by Polly and Margaret's go by Molly. It gets harder than that. And then there are the abbreviations like "Jos" for Joseph, "Wm" for William and "Thos" for Thomas. And finally, there are spelling differences like Steven for Stephen. If you are avid about genealogy, you will learn them all over time.

A situation I see quite often is a family having two or more children with the same first names. I some cases their middle names are different like John Fitzgerald, John Paul, or John Boy. And we must not forget that George Forman and his wife gave all 10 of their boys the same first name as George.

Another case where a family might have more than one child with the same first is when the first child with that name died young and the family chose to reuse the name. Or there was a remarriage and the new spouse wanted to reuse the name. I have seen this done three times in one family.

If I have not made the case for recording middle names, just think about searching through a list of John Smiths all born about the same year (yes, it happens). Having that middle name or at least a middle initial can quickly narrow down the list.

Another thing that affects surnames is cultural rules. In some cultures, the last name is inherited from the mother's surname and the father's name is added as a middle name. There are other variations on this which make paying attention to the actual chain of ancestor easier if you know the rules and harder if you do not. There is also the case way back when surnames barely existed and you were basically given one which might not even hint at who your real parents were. This practice existed in tribal areas as well as aristocracy of Europe.

Missing Given Names

If you do not know a given name, please just leave it blank. Refrain from entering "unknown", "male", or "female". These are wasted keystrokes and more importantly they confuse the search matching algorithms. It causes you extra work to remove them from records you get for others.

Like most others, if an infant does not have a given name, I simply leave it blank since a name might turn up in later research. However, in cases where documentation states that an infant died before being named, I give them a given name of "unnamed".

Maiden Names (birth surname)

Tracing mothers is much harder to do because of the tradition of changing a maiden surname to a married surname. In my records, I list all females by their maiden names with their married names as alternates. If I do not know the maiden name, I leave it blank or use the married name and add "Mrs." as the prefix so people will know that the maiden name is not known.

Yes, there are cases where the maiden name is already the same as the married name. Ask anyone from Boston named Sullivan or anyone from Los Angeles names Rodrigues. In this case I add a note that the wife's maiden name was already the same as their spouse's surname. Linking in with their parents also helps to clear up that mystery.

There are also cases where you do not know the woman's given name, but you do know the married surname. In this case I use the married surname, add a prefix or "Mrs." and leave the given name blank.

Most software programs do allow a person to have multiple names over their lifetime. The software I use has an "alternate names" feature.

Another reason to use maiden names in your tree is if you are trying to get help from others on your tree. Someone may have a daughter that they can't trace and if you have that maiden name and birth date name published you might just get a match. I certainly have resolved some of my brick walls this way.

Tip: It is better if a woman registers their DNA and their tree in their maiden name. In genealogy we focus on birth names for every person.

Nicknames

I will often put a person's nickname in parentheses or quotes after their given name. Ex: John "Jack" F. Kennedy. This helps with traceability to records where one record used the given name and another used the nickname. And, in my case my family tree software will use names in quotes as the person's name in narratives. Kind of a nice feature. I do wish the world could standardize on this because I often find myself removing other people's punctuation marks to put in simple quotes, or in moving the nickname to be before the middle names.

Name Suffixes

Some suffixes can help you in tracing a male surname by signaling that the person had a father or son with the same given name. Examples: Senior, Junior, the 3rd… Other suffixes are also good with stating a person's standing in their society like Duke of Earl, The Great… or PHD, DDS, Esq CPA… Every clue helps.

Dates

It is best to record dates in a format of Day, Month, Year. Ex: 4 Jul 1776. Yes, we are not taught to do it this way, but which is easier to understand: 8/4/21 or 4 Aug 1621? It gets confusing if you transpose the month and day or do not know which century the record is for.

Sometimes you will see a "Bef" or "Aft" in front of a date. This is a case where the exact date is not known but some other documents such as a census record, child's birth record, probate will, or newspaper article prove the person was alive or dead at a certain date. So, if my will is proven on 22 oct 2121, but my date of death was not known, it could be entered as "bef 22 oct 2121". Similarly, if someone found Jesus's baptism record but didn't know when he was born, they could enter a birthdate of "bef 0028".

Again, we don't want to guess at a date without facts to get us close to the real date. For example, if we don't know when a person died but knew when their last child was born, we still don't really know when they died with enough accuracy. In this case it's better to just leave the date of death blank and wait for better facts to be found.

Birth Dates

A person's birth data tells when a person was born. Every record should have a birth date. Imagine a person with no birth date. What century were they born in? Wouldn't it be better to know at least that?

The birth date can be used by your family tree tool to identify duplicates which is a great help. I cannot tell you how many times my genealogy software has popped up an alert telling me I have a similar person already in my database and they could be the same person I am entering right now. The birth date is also used by search tools to help look at the right sets of records.

I use some rules of thumb to give an estimated birth date to people who do not have one. First, it starts with a prefix of "About", "Before", or "After". This tells everyone that the date is not exact. Then, if it is a spouse, I use their spouse's birth year. Ex: "About 1450". This is probably within 10 years of accurate. If it is a child or parent, I use a 20-year difference. This is usually enough to indicate the person is not duplicate.

If you have data about the person's siblings, you might adjust your estimate up or down to fit a gap in the birth order, if it makes sense to do so.

Later, if you find a census and cemetery record with a closer estimated date, you can modify it. The closer you get to the real date the better. Try it, you might be surprised at how often it helps and how close your guesses really are.

Also, it's best to record dates in a format of Day, Month, Year. Ex: 4 Jul 1776. Yes, we are not taught to do it this way, but which is easier to understand: 8/4/21 or 4 Aug 1621? It gets confusing if you transpose the month and day or do not know which century the record is for.

It is still common practice to drop unwanted babies at a church. When this occurs, the church will usually put the infant in an orphanage for adoption. Putting a church name as a birth location should mean the baby was actually born in that church, not dropped off for adoption. It helps to be clear.

Baptism Dates

Many people like to record baptism dates. If you do this, please try to have the location stated clearly. The word "Civil" would infer it was conducted at home. But "St Louis" is ambiguous. Was this the city or a church such the Saint Louis Basilica? It is better to state it clearly.

Marriage Dates

In cases where people have married multiple times, marriage dates help in sorting out which children belong to which parents. Whenever possible I try to enter a marriage date. I do not like to estimate these because there is uncertainty where you do not know if there are more spouses until you find one. If you feel you need to estimate a marriage date, pick a date just before the first known child and preface it with "about".

Putting the right children with the right parents is important and it gets tough if one or the other has remarried and has had more children. It is an area I personally have been affected by too many times. If you are trying to sort out DNA matches and common ancestors, working your way up the right tree makes a difference. Look at birth dates and marriage dates to make sure that everything is right.

On another thought, you will find records that appear to have someone born or married in the town of "Civil". For example, one of my father's on-line records says he was born in Civil, Methuen, MA. I know that it is not true because he was born at home in my grandparent's house in Methuen, MA. What is happening is people enter the word "civil" into the birth or marriage field to record that there is no actual birth or marriage record. These people were likely born at home or married by common law and never had formal records created for the event. My recommendation is to put this sort of information in the notes and not confuse the location

Death Dates

Death dates help in the same ways as marriage dates and for finding gravestone data. In many cases only the death date is known for gravestone data. However, once you know the right cemetery, you can peruse around it and often find other relatives that you are looking for.

A bad habit I see often is putting other information in the date field like "Dead" or Deceased". To me this causes more problems than help. Date field are for dates. Even worst is stating the burial location as "unknown". This is implicitly inferring that it will always be unknown while it might only be unknown to you.

One other bad habit I see is people entering "Dead" or Deceased" in the death location field. It almost makes sense if the person died in the last 20 years, but I see this going back 200+ years. I say leave it blank if you do not know the location

Locations of deaths should be accurate and unambiguous. For example, someone who died in Salt Lake should be recorded as "Salt Lake City" so it is clear that they did not die in the great Salt Lake.

And, if a person died at sea, it would be nice to know which ocean and maybe a reference point like "off Georges Bank".

Living People

Information about living people should be kept private. If you upload your data to a public website, which most of us do, have your export program hide living people so nothing will be display anything about them – as if they do not exist. Even the smallest clues can help the wrong people find more details about them which they can use to exploit for conducting identity fraud. How often have you used your mother's maiden name or your father's middle name as the answer to a security question?

Protecting living people's privacy IS important. Be careful with what you know about a person's identity and who you share it with. History has proven that sharing a person's heritage can have unintended results.

A downside of protecting identity is some of your DNA matches might post a tree of only one of the parents or grandparents. The match you might be looking for might be in the part of the family that is not posted.

Event Locations

Recording event locations helps to put a person at a place on the earth. Having this data will help you know where to go to possibly find deeper data about a person. Examples are the places where a person was born, married, lived, or buried. If you do not know the exact location, you can record the part you do know such as the county, state, country. Or prefix a location with the word "of" to indicate you do not know but they most recently were from this location. If you do not know at all, leave it blank to fill in some other day.

I like to spell out locations and avoid abbreviations. The genealogical community is international, and it is a lot easier for others if they don't have to learn that "ME" means "Maine, USA". You never know when you or someone else might want to visit a location to find deeper data or experience what life might have been like there.

Also, names of places change over time. I like to use the name of the time the event occurred. For example, Massachusetts was Massachusetts Bay Colony of Colonial England before it became Massachusetts, USA. And the City of Boston was first called Shawmut long ago. And the USA did not exist prior to 1776.

Yes, it does cause someone to learn something about history. But it also helps find the older records. The people who created the records had no idea that the name of their town or country was going to change later in time. People in New Amsterdam certainly did not know that their town would become New York City. And what if your ancestors are from Constantinople?

And did you know that Maine was once part of Massachusetts for a few years?

Recording locations should stay simple like a postal address. Avoid adding "village of", "township of", "county/parish of", "state of". This extra text makes the location longer and can be confusing to search engines. Keep it simple!

Country names should be included but the country's name can still be controversial. Do you use the Americanized name or the country's formal name? Using the formal name or their formal abbreviation can help people in other countries find your records. For example, did you know the Japan is actually Nippon? Germany is actually Deutschland? And England is actually Angleterre? The United States is known as Etas Unite in many countries?

A pet peeve of mine is cemetery name information. Who knew that a single cemetery could be recorded by many different names. I say stick to its formal name. This makes it a lot easier if you want to see a list of everyone buried in that cemetery. A similar problem happens with church names.

Event Dates

Event dates are good to have. In the case of multiple spouses, marriage dates help sort out which children go with which spouse. Immigration dates can help with finding immigration records which often contain the place where the person was from, who traveled with them and where they were heading. Death dates help find wills which can contain more details of a person's descendants and what they things of value they passed on to their survivors.

Spouses

Why enter the spouses? Well in the direction of ancestors going up your tree it is obvious; these people are your ancestors. But on the descendant's side, knowing whether it is a spouse of your descendant or spouse of your ancestor's descendant, you need them to help sort out whose children are whose when there are multiple spouses. In the case of the male spouses, you need them to track the children of that couple. And, you are adding one more verification that you have traced the right couple in your tree.

Also, someone else might be tracking that spouse's name and has clues to who some of your ancestors or descendants are. So, at the very least, it is worth it to record them just to advertise them in hopes someone will find your tree and help you out. Or maybe you will be helping them out, you will never know if you do not take the time to record those spouses.

Matching Duplicates

When matching up people who might be duplicates you need to take extra care. It is quite possible to have two people with the same name born in the same year and month, and even in the same town but have different parents. And considering two people as being the same person just because they both married the same spouse can also be deceiving because a spouse might die, and the brother or sister of that spouse might marry the surviving spouse. Check the marriage dates. Each person needs to be validated.

Notes

Most genealogy software has a place for notes. Some will break out places for different kinds of notes such as general (obits and such), Medical (cause of death and such) and Research (things that need more work).

Please put your notes in the note's places. It is frustrating when notes are tucked in with other data such as "Date of Death: Died unmarried" or "Spouse: Unknown". My least favorite is adding notes to names like

"Name: John Q. Public / Farmer". Is this person named Public or Farmer? Or was he a farmer?

DNA is a great tool for helping you find your relatives. To start, it can tell you if you are related to your father's side (Y-dna) or your mother's side (mt-dna). This narrows down ½ of your tree that you need to search in for a common ancestor. Then, based on how much DNA you match with another person, it can narrow down how far back in your tree you need to look at.

However, this data is not as exact in predicting the distance due to events such as half-brothers or half-sisters. And it can get confusing if ancestors in your tree have married back into the family tree such as two first cousins marrying and having offspring. This was common in royalty and isolated communities. Another common but less confusing event is when a spouse dies, and the person marries their spouse's brother, sister, or cousin. This is not as confusing to the DNA but still can add a level of complexity.

A short story. Centimorgans (CMs) represent the lengths of common segments of DNA. If you have no common segments, you are not related. The more segments you have, the closer you are related. The actual calculation is tough because males and females have differences and that are differences based on the genetic markers themselves. I like to keep it simple and stick with halving the centimorgans for each generation.

The name Centimorgan was given in honor of Thomas Hunt Morgan, a pioneer in chromosome study back in the early 1900s.

Some websites have a feature that suggests ancestors for your tree based on trees from your DNA matches. In most cases I have found the suggested ancestors to be correct. However, I recently found one case where the suggested route to the common ancestor was defying validation. Something was rotten in Demark! My paper tree diverged away from the suggested ancestor instead of converging to it. Since both me and the other person clearly had shared DNA that suggested a common ancestor at the 5th grand parent level on my father's side, I believe that either an out of marriage conception or an adoption had occurred. The other person has only filled in two generations in their tree so I will be contacting them to find other surnames that we both share DNA with. Or it could be a case of hidden adoption. In either case, the DNA will eventually help uncover the truth (postscript, it was a hidden adoption).

In several cases I have found that the suggested route to the common ancestor led to the wrong sibling, I can understand this since siblings tend to share the same DNA.

A side story. Recently I had a 1st cousin pop up as a DNA match. Since I know who all my 1st cousins are, I was intrigued. She contacted me before I had a chance to contact her. Since 1st cousins share a common grandparent, we exchanged details about our grandparents. She later contacted me to say her grandmother and my grandfather grew up in the same town. This made him a prime suspect. Digger deeper she found a newspaper article listing attendees for a 10-year high school reunion with both of our grandparents attending. Nine months later her mother was born. We believe we found the smoking gun. My grandfather never mentioned a fourth child, and it is possible he never knew.

Personally, I find exploring my DNA tree more interesting than my paper tree. And there seems to be a trend of others who have turned to following their DNA and incorporating those people into their paper trail tree.

Using your Parents DNA

I have access to my mom's DNA on Ancestry.com and I can look at her matches. This is helpful because in theory her matches are different from my dad's. In my case that holds true only back 5 generations. Farther back there is overlap since my mom and dad were 5th cousins. They did not know this when they met. It was discovered when we started taking a serious look at our family genealogy much later in in the winter of their lives. The first clue we had was a gravestone in Freeport Maine that had surnames names from both my mom's and dad's trees. A later clue was in Hull's Cove Maine where a graveyard contained many people from both sides of the family.

An interesting thing I noticed was that my mom had names in her matches that I did not have in mine. Also, I had names in my match list that she did not have in hers. This is because you do not inherit all the DNA of your parents. Unless you are exceedingly rare identical twins, everyone has unique DNA. The good news is that her matches helped me solve some brick walls in my tree. Maybe I would have solved them eventually without her DNA, but it happened faster with it.

Also, as I look at my mom's matches, I can see that her first cousins are my second cousins, which is an important difference. Everything is shifted by one generation so her first cousins share about 815 CMs with her and my 2nd cousins share about 255 CMs with me. That gap gets smaller each generation back on an asymptote curve such that her 8 CM matches are my 8 CM matches.

Using your Children's DNA

I have access to my daughter's DNA on Ancestry.com. Similarly, when reviewing my mother's perspective, I must consciously adjust my viewpoint to align with hers. Her mother's side matches to her are my wife's family and father's side matches to her are my family. She does not have the advantage of knowing which grandparent the match relates to like her mom, and I do. So, just for that reason alone I have to say that having your parents' DNA might be more valuable than having your children.

My mom had matches that I did not have, and I had matches that she did not have. In the case of my daughter, I have matches she does not have, especially way back in generations, and she has only a few father's side matches that I do not have, two to be exact.

Another observation I made was that she has 16,739 matches while I have 39,954 matches. I speculate that this is influenced by her mom's side having very few matches, the generation shift, and fewer people having fewer children. By generation shift, I mean the drop off for the very distant matches.

Adoptions

Adoptions have been around for many years, and they are not always identified in people's family trees.

In my family tree there are adoptions. Most have been cases that stayed in the family such as both parents dying and their children being raised by another family relative.

DNA will reveal them, but a paper trail may be impossible to find to support a proper validation. The easiest to find are cases where both the parent and child have posted their DNA online. Those almost find themselves.

Adoptions that occurred several generations back are much harder to resolve. DNA will get you to the right area but finding the exact person takes a process of ruling out everyone else. A spreadsheet with names and notes is the best tool I have found, and the answer may not come for years.

A side story: I received an email several years back from a young lady whose DNA said I was her biological father (not a scam). I was the right age and came from the right small town and had the same first name as her mom had told her she remembered. Only problem was that it was not _my_ DNA she was comparing to. My assumption is that she had become so excited to find a match that she had not taken the time to verify her data. She sent me here DNA profile data and I quickly found that she was 90 % Italian. And since I had no Italian, not even a trace, it was not a match. I do like Italian food though. And my stepfather was Italian. Capeesh?

So why did her software say it was a match? Well, I did have a distant match with her mother, probably 6 or 7 generations back. But what she did not know was that the amount of shared DNA was nowhere near large enough (you need >3000cm to match to be a parent of a child) and the few matching segments were all from her mother's side (mt-dna). Hopefully, she will someday find her father. I am not sure if her mom might have been referencing a different town in a different state. I do not remember anyone with my first name being near my age in my town.

Websites

There are many websites that will allow you to take a DNA test and build a tree for collaborating with others. Most also let you download your DNA results for upload from one website to another. Be aware that most people seem to stick with one website which means the data you are searching for might exist but is on a different website than yours. I have my tree on several of the bigger websites and a couple of specialized "niche" websites.

Creating a tree that maximizes your ability to be found in searches and follows the general rules is important.

An anomaly I see often is not necessarily incorrect but as I research a person's connection to me, I sometimes find an alternate route to a different common ancestor. Most website's algorithms can only present one route at a time and due to cross marriages, there can be multiple routes and multiple common ancestors.

Some websites have a nice feature that will suggest ancestors for you. Pay close attention to the word "evaluate" in the suggested list. Do research to verify each connection. I will usually start at the top and work downward. If I get stuck, I go to the bottom and work upward. And sometimes I might end up evaluating a name in the middle. Even then, occasionally I cannot make all the connections with verified records. In that case I save the suggested ancestors as "speculative" and do not link them into my tree. My speculation ancestors often do end up connecting to my tree later in life when more data has come available.

Some of my speculative entries come from my noticing a certain surname, middle name, town name, or just a gut feeling that they might link into my tree someday. So far most have.

Most of my speculative entries are also people who are in or likely in 2 degrees of separation from my real tree. I try to keep my database to only people who connect with me in some way. If I find myself wandering off to people who are not likely related to me, I stop there. Having a database of only people who relate to me is a big plus when trying to research a new DNA match.

Also, be aware that the dates in the DNA matches are often "rounded" which can make then seem off by a few years. Example "July 1799" might round to 1800. Or, if the source record is using a date like "from 1750 to 1780" or "before 1601" might round to a year that is few years up or down from what you have.

Hint: Most websites use adaptive technology to present their data. If you have a wide screen, set it to a high resolution you should be able to see the person and more generations above them when viewing someone's tree. Narrower/lower resolution can reduce the number of generations in view at one time.

The website tools are improving every year and more people ae getting their DNA tested, posting their trees, and interacting with others to grow their trees. This continuous churn means it is well worth watching for new DNA matches and trees that have been expanded.

Color Coding and Adding Notes for Matches

If the website offers it, one of the things I like to do is color code my DNA matches by group so I can keep up with who I have traced (light green), who I have recorded (blue), who I need to research (yellow), who is not yet traced (red) and whose tree is private (black). I have at least everyone with higher than 30CMs coded. Most of my "not traced" connections are people with no tree, a private tree, a tree with only a few people recorded, or it was just too hard to find a match in their tree.

The great benefit of color coding your matches comes from periodically checking to see if a match has created their tree or updated their tree. I use the "notes" section to record the date of my visit and what I found. Most of it in note like "no tree", "tree is only self", tree is all private", "no paternal or no maternal side", and "no match found". The date helps me decide if it's time to research again. I like to wait a year.

Integrity

Not all family trees have the same integrity. Sometimes it appears as if parts of someone's tree have been "whitewashed" to remove certain relatives or change dates to fit social norms of the times. Or more commonly are people linking in parents that are not correct. To ensure high integrity, it is best to validate your tree using physical records such as birth certificates, baptism records, death certificates, census records, obituaries, gravestones, family bibles and such. It is not perfect, but it is better than none. Just because someone else's tree says two people are related, does not necessarily make it true.

I do tend to trust data given to me from people that is about who their parents or grandparents are. This tends to be quite accurate, especially if they know if they were adopted or not. Data from people close to the source is usually more accurate.

I have seen lots of errors in other people's trees. Watch carefully at:

- Children born before their parents were – could be a missing generation
- Children born after their mother died - could be the father remarried

- Birth certifications in multiple states – not sure what causes this but I have seen it several times
- Stepparent presented as birth parent
- Long dead ancestors set as private
- Parents who do not seem to fit at all – wishful thinking?

My father always said if you are going to do something, do it well. A little bit of patience and diligence will help you build an accurate family tree.

Also, does your paper trail match your DNA trail? I have found several places in mine that show divergences. This is likely due to adoptions or out of marriage births that are not noted as such.

Brick Walls

Sometimes you just can't find enough data to link a parent and child or vice versa. This is what we call a "brick wall". It stops your progress right at that spot. In recent years DNA and more on-line data records have helped me resolve many of my brick walls. It used to be I had to plan a vacation to a town so I could do the research. That worked out well most of the time and I still have a list of places to go in the future.

DNA can build a good case, especially if you have other collaborating data, but it is still hard to be 100% conclusive. But new information is being discovered all the time. My ancestor Stephen Hopkins died in 1644, and it wasn't until 1989 that his baptism record was discovered in England.

You will have brick walls. I am still waiting for the first person to trace their tree back to Adam & Eve come forward to say they have no brick walls in their tree. My last count on my tree was over 1000 dead ends. How do I know, I keep a spreadsheet of my ancestors by year and place of birth with a code showing when do not have parents. BTW, this same spread sheet is handy for keeping track of which ancestors are common ancestors for my DNA matches. I count them for each ancestor. And it becomes obvious which ancestors are likely valid for me and which one might not be.

Another thought about why we try so hard to get our family history right. There is a saying that people die twice, once when they stop breathing and again when nobody remembers them. As I add each person's information to my database, I take the time to read it and imagine how their life might have been. Again, it is the stories that make each person interesting.

Conflicting Source Data

As you dig deeper you will undoubtable come across conflicting source data. One source says one fact and another source has a conflicting fact. It is not so bad when it is a day off or by a few months, or a location off by a few towns. But, when it's different parents or different children, it gets concerning. It all comes down to who do <u>you</u> believe is right. This used to be a tough problem, but DNA has helped to solve it.

However, it might take a lot of research and communication to figure out the DNA part. And there is always the possibility of adoption or deliberate falsification of records driven by cultural rules of the time.

So, what do you do? For me, I record the alternate facts and stop my tree at that person. Then, I wait until I have a few DNA matches that collaborate with which one is correct. Hopefully, being in the winter phase of my life, that data might not arrive until after I pass on to the next world. Of course, once there I will know the answer, but I will have no way to tell anyone in the flesh and blood world what it is. Sorry Charlie.

One thing you should be aware of is that most often you are viewing other people's trees and there can be many trees covering overlapping sets of people in your tree. This means that just because one tree ends, another tree might continue and may have the information you are searching for. It also means that you can find conflicting data between trees that you will need to resolve. And, some people do not include other spouses, which makes linking to/from that tree more difficult.

When I come across conflicting data, I try to look at each objectively and apply some critical thinking to see which version has a higher probability of being right. Familysearch.org includes a quality indicator on their profile pages that can help. Examining dates, places, name spelling, middle names in comparison to other close relatives can give you clues. Also be aware that some mistakes get propagated to other trees since we all tend to copy each other's work. If possible, don't be the person who copies bad data.

Data Sources

Data sources are important. Do not just record that you found the data on the internet, or it was sent to you from so and so at this email address. The Internet and email addresses are ever changing and are not reliable over time. What you should be recording is the document name and where it is located. Your tree should be traceable back to the source data such as birth, marriage and death certificates, census records, church records, family bibles, local newspapers, court records, wills, obituaries, cemeteries, and such.

Lucky for all of us the Church of Latter-Day Saints has made it their mission to find and record family records all over the world. You can and should thank them for this effort. Their genealogy libraries are open to all to explore with the largest being in Salt Lake City, Utah. I am not sure why they do it, but I am thankful that they do.

Contacting Others

Be careful in contacting people. They can be highly suspicious that you are a scammer or may not have gotten over the loss of the person you are inquiring about. Best to go slow and build a relationship. I like to explain the gap in my tree that I am trying to fill in and ask if they might be able to help.

FamilySearch.org

FamilySearch.org is one of my "go to" tools for researching. It does take some experience to get good at using it. For example, although it automatically considers phonetic spellings of surnames, it takes first names literally. You might need to try different spellings of first names to find the person you are looking for. And even if it comes up with the ever disappointing "no records found", the addition of a middle initial or full middle name can often make a difference to finding records.

How this site handles public records is great. If find a person in a public record (at least the newer USA ones), you can click on a name, and the site will find other related documents for that person such as census, birth, marriage, and death records to help you be certain you have the right person.

If you build a tree in family search, please make sure it is accurate. And, if you have the answer to an error in someone else's tree, please take the time to suggest it or update it and provide the reason why you think your data is correct (example: give link to a data source such as Wikipedia or FindAGrave). I do this often in hopes that it will help others.

Currently a lot of the trees in Family Search are "islands" that don't connect to other trees. Over time people have been connecting trees together to grow a proverbial master tree. I like this, it gives one place were controversial connections might get resolved.

FindAGrave.com

Graves.com is another of my favorite search tools. Data there is usually quite accurate since it comes directly off gravestones, and it has typically been edited by close family members. Some people include obituaries which can be quite helpful in tracing parents and children's names. And some people include family photos which help with the person's story.

Note that its search algorithm relies heavily on the surname and date of death. Do not be afraid to try maiden names since they are often recorded on the records. And, just like the days when you had to roam the graveyards to gather information, I often find spouse names and dates in the photos of gravestones where no other records seem to be on-line.

Also, look at who has left flowers. They are often close relatives and could be good genealogical contact for more information if you need it.

And, look around the graveyard for potential other relatives.

Consider building memorials for your closest relatives, those you have certain data for. Your siblings and cousins can also create memorials and link theirs to yours or vice versa.

Gedmatch.com

Gedmatch.com is a "techy" site that lets you do things like compare your DNA to DNA with ancient people, compare your DNA with your DNA matches, find common ancestors in your family trees, and other things. I exported a separate ancestor tree for each of my four grandparents and loaded them separately to the website. This was initially necessary because my ancestor tree exceeded their upload size limit. Later I realized it made it easy to know which part of the family I am researching. You need tricks like this when your tree gets to be over 10,000 people.

Obituaries

Obituaries can be a goldmine of information. Many times, they will give the names of the parents, spouse, brothers, sisters, children, and more. It is well worth searching for them, especially when you find your path forward is blocked.

They are also a great source of stories about the person. Many times, people will include a short biography of the person's life.

Census Records

Census records are great for validating parent and child relationships. And it will sometimes reveal the name of a grandparent living with one of their children's families. However, they are not clear if a child is DNA related or adopted.

Mistakes

People make mistakes. It is not a perfect world. Some things that look like mistakes are not technically mistakes such as changes in surname spelling, use of a married name in place of a maiden name, or use of a middle name or nickname as a first name. But others like linking a grandchild to a grandparent (missing a generation), entering birth dates off by 100 years (1901 instead of 1801), and linking children to wrong parents (parent died and spouse remarried) are all preventable if we all take the time to check out our work.

There is another set of common issues that are hard to classify as mistakes, but they sure look like something is wrong. These are the cases where a person gets baptized before they were born, baptized a place too far away for the timeframe (ex: born in the 1600s in Massachusetts and baptized the same day in England), buried before they died, or buried in a place to far away for the time frame (ex: died in the 1600s in Virginia and buried in England the next day).

Loading GEDCOMs from others can create a lot of mistakes in seconds if the data fields are not mapped correctly. Always save a backup file before doing a GEDCOM import. Also use find and replace to fix what you can.

Computer crashes can also cause errors. Backing up your data often will help reduce the impact.

Applications

How do I keep my public tree data separated from my work-in-progress tree data? I use a family tree application on my home computer for my working data, and I will export my well documented ancestor tree to public sites a few times each year. It would only cause confusion in the genealogical community if I were to publish my unverified work. And I have hundreds of speculation records stored just in case I can link them into my tree someday. I do not need people asking about those records since I cannot explain how they fit into my tree yet. Keeping the two sets of data separate solves these issues for me. I recommend you do the same.

Many people ask me which application I prefer, and I say I am no expert since I have essentially used the same application for many years. I am used to how it works and know most of its quarks. If you must know, it is Millennia Legacy Deluxe Edition <now at 10.0 version>. It has worked well for me, so I have never tried any others. Also. It's free. As a rule, I use only free sources and the only money out of my pocket for this hobby was for my DNA test.

GEDCOMs

There is a standard file format for sharing genealogical data between systems called GEDCOM. It will allow you to upload your tree to other genealogical websites and exchange trees with others. However, it will also let you move and lot of bogus data if you do not review the data carefully. It is always best to make sure all the people in your tree can be traced to some sort of documentation. It only takes one wrong connection to set your tree off onto an incorrect tangent and have you spend hours documenting people that are not actually part of your real tree.

Publishing Your Tree

When I first started building my family tree, I had ideas about publishing it someday so it could be stored in libraries everywhere for others to enjoy. My great aunt did just that and her 588-page book titled "Descendants of Thomas Brewer". It is in the New England Historic Genealogical Society's library. I might still do this someday for the descendants of John Mackey.

But what I discovered along the way is that my tree is big. It is too big to email someone, and it is too big to print out for a friend. I have 85,000 people documented in my tree and that is small compared to some who have 250,000+.

I used to publish my whole tree but as it grown to be too big, I now only publish my ancestors. This is great for two reasons. One is my primary goal is growing my ancestor tree. The other reason is that I was getting consumed with questions about distant descendants that I could not answer since those came for my DNA matches. Best I could do I tell people how they fit into my tree.

You often see people with a chart style tree showing their family all on one page. This works well for one or two generations but quickly becomes unmanageable as you add generations. I can print out a "fan" chart with 5 generations on it, but it takes 16 pieces of standard paper that I must tape together after. I did this once for a family reunion and gave up printing paper after that. Now I print to PDF and display it on my big screen TV. However, PDFs have a size limit so my whole tree does not fit. And it can be too big to email.

You can create a nice book but if you have a big tree, it becomes too big to bind. In the big picture you are better off focusing on just descendants of one ancestor to keep it manageable.

Another problem that has plagued me is the fact that the data keeps evolving. Of course, new descendants are getting added all the time, which is normal life. But I also occasionally will discover new ancestors and I might need to correct problems in the tree that I did not even know I had. Again, the quest for perfection holds me back. This booklet will likely be published before my completed family tree book ever does.

Conclusion

Maybe it's just a pastime or a curiosity, or maybe God told you to do it, whatever your motivation is for creating a family tree, please do it right and share your results with others. I hope you found my short book to be helpful in getting you started off on the right footing.

If you are passionately interested in genealogy, consider attending the annual RootsTech Connect conference where you can meet and hear the experts talk about the latest advancements in roots tracing. I have been attending online for years.